THE ROADMAP FOR

CONTENT CREATORS

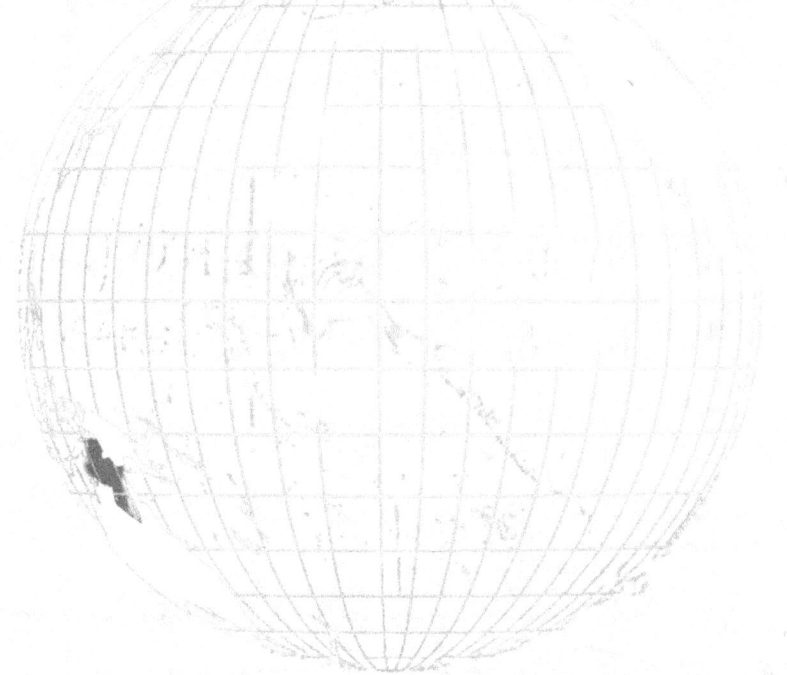

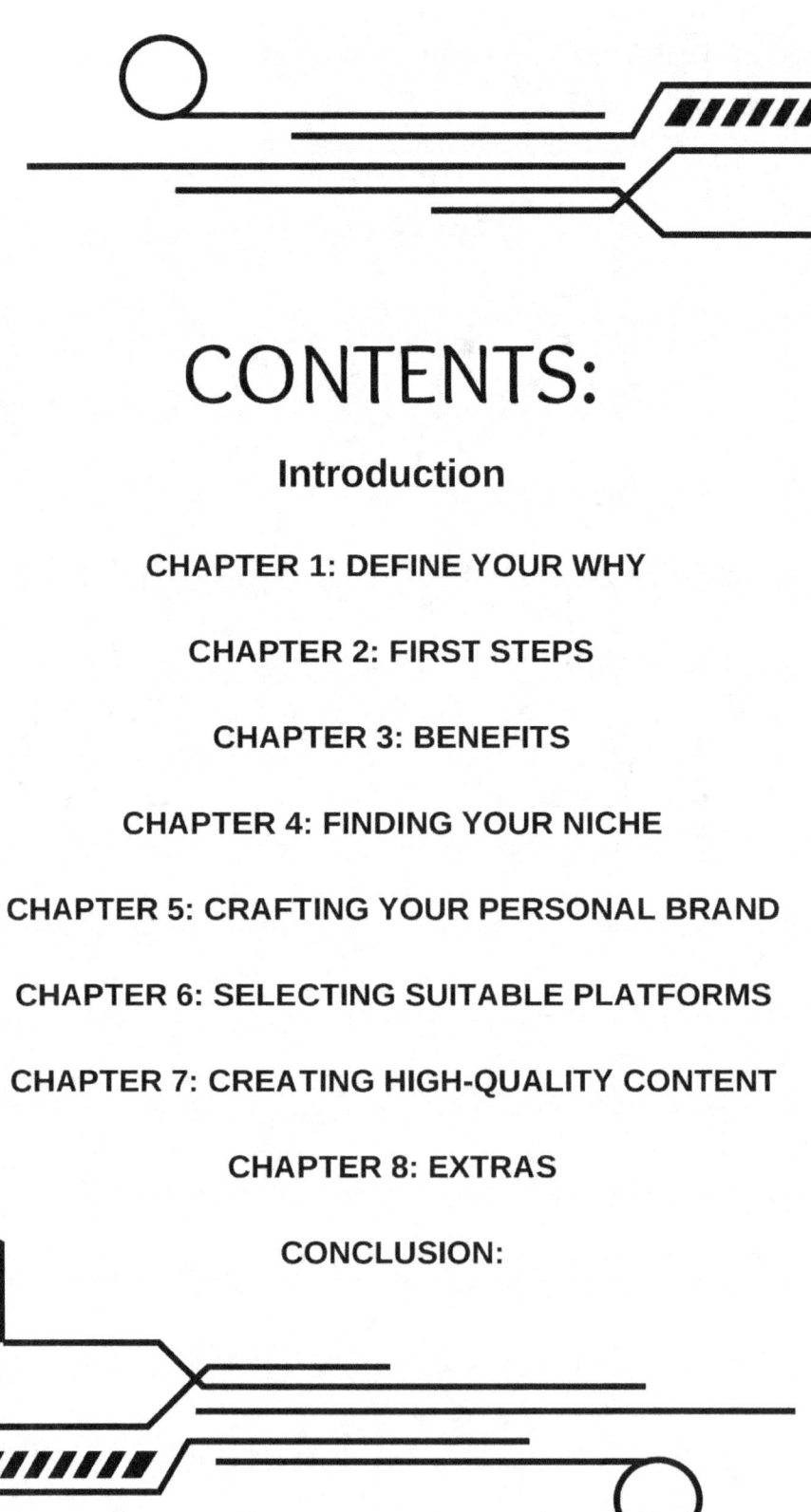

CONTENTS:

Introduction

Introduction

Welcome!!

Welcome to "The Roadmap for Content Creators. Your Adventure Awaits: Conquer the Digital Frontier" your ultimate guide to becoming a successful online content creator. Whether you're just starting out or looking to refine your existing skills, this workbook is designed to help you navigate the ever-evolving digital landscape and make your mark in the world of online content.

In today's digital age, content creation is more than just a hobby—it's a powerful way to share your voice, build a community, and even create a sustainable career. From bloggers and vloggers to social media influencers and podcasters, online content creators are shaping the future of media and communication.

How to Use This Workbook

You're about to embark on an exciting adventure into the world of online content creation. This journey will be filled with challenges and opportunities, but with the right mindset and tools, you can overcome any obstacle and achieve your dreams.
So, let's get started!

This workbook is structured to provide a blend of theoretical knowledge, practical exercises, and strategic insights. Each section is carefully crafted to guide you through different aspects of content creation, from understanding the digital landscape to developing technical skills and building a robust online presence.

Turn the page and begin your journey to becoming a masterful online content creator. The digital world is waiting for your unique contribution—let's make it extraordinary.

Chapter 1:

Define Your Why

Being an online content creator involves the creation and sharing of digital content across various platforms such as social media, blogs, videos, and podcasts. As an online content creator, you have the opportunity to express your creativity, share your knowledge, connect with others, and potentially even monetize your content. This dynamic field allows individuals to build their personal brand, engage with a global audience, and contribute to online communities.

Benefits of Creating Content Online

This book serves as a comprehensive guide and workbook specifically designed to assist beginners in their journey to becoming successful online content creators. It provides step-by-step guidance, practical exercises, and valuable insights to navigate the process effectively.

Ultimately, this book empowers beginners with the knowledge, tools, and resources necessary to kickstart their online content creation journey and increase their chances of success in this exciting and rapidly evolving field.

First Steps

Take a few minutes to reflect on your personal and professional goals. What are your passions, interests, and hobbies? What topics do you feel strongly about?

Write your answer here...

Consider the benefits of creating content online. What do you hope to gain by becoming an online content creator? Do you want to share your knowledge, connect with others, or build a personal brand?

Write your answer here...

Write down your why. Based on your reflections, write a brief statement that explains why you want to become an online content creator. This statement should be personal and meaningful to you.

Write your answer here...

Example for an aspiring travel blogger

"My why is to inspire others to explore the world and experience new cultures, while also learning more about myself and my place in the world. I believe that travel has the power to open our minds, connect us with others, and make the world a better place, and I want to share that message through my content."

Remember, your why statement should be unique to you, and should reflect your personal goals and values. Use this exercise as a starting point to define your why, and refer back to it whenever you need motivation or inspiration to create content.

The Benefits

Creative Expression

Online content creation provides a platform for you to unleash your creativity and showcase your unique voice and ideas. Whether it's through writing, photography, videography, or other mediums, you have the freedom to express yourself and share your passions with the world.

Empower your content creation journey.

Knowledge Sharing

Creating content online allows you to share your expertise, skills, and experiences with others. You can educate and inspire your audience, helping them learn and grow in various areas of interest.

Global Reach

The internet offers a vast audience base, allowing you to connect with people from around the world. Your content has the potential to make a positive impact, spark conversations, and inspire individuals from diverse backgrounds.

Building a Personal Brand

As an online content creator, you have the opportunity to develop a personal brand that reflects your values, style, and niche. This branding can lead to recognition, credibility, and increased opportunities for collaborations and partnerships.

Networking and Community Building

Creating content online enables you to connect with like-minded individuals, industry professionals, and potential collaborators. Building a network and engaging with your audience fosters meaningful relationships and opens doors to new opportunities.

Chapter 3:
The Benefits
Continued

Your Adventure
Awaits: Conquer
the Digital Frontier

Monetization Possibilities

Content creation can serve as a source of income. By growing your audience and establishing a loyal following, you can explore various monetization avenues, such as brand partnerships, sponsored content, advertising, merchandise sales, or offering products and services.

Flexibility and Independence

Embrace the freedom of online content creation, where you set the pace and shape your creative journey. Enjoy the flexibility, independence, and limitless opportunities to express your passions and build a fulfilling career on your terms. Unleash your creativity and unlock your potential today.

Finding Your Niche

Brainstorm your interests, skills, and expertise.

Write your answer here...

Research popular topics within those areas and identify gaps or underserved niches.

Write your answer here...

Define your target audience by considering demographics, interests, and needs.	
Are they male or female?	
How old are they?	
Single? Married? Kids?	
What do they do for work?	
Where do they live?	
What worries do they have?	
What are they frustrated with?	
What are their values in life?	
Why will they want to visit your site?	

Research popular topics within those areas and identify gaps or underserved niches.

Write your answer here...

Create a Venn diagram or list to find the intersection between your passions and the audience's interests.

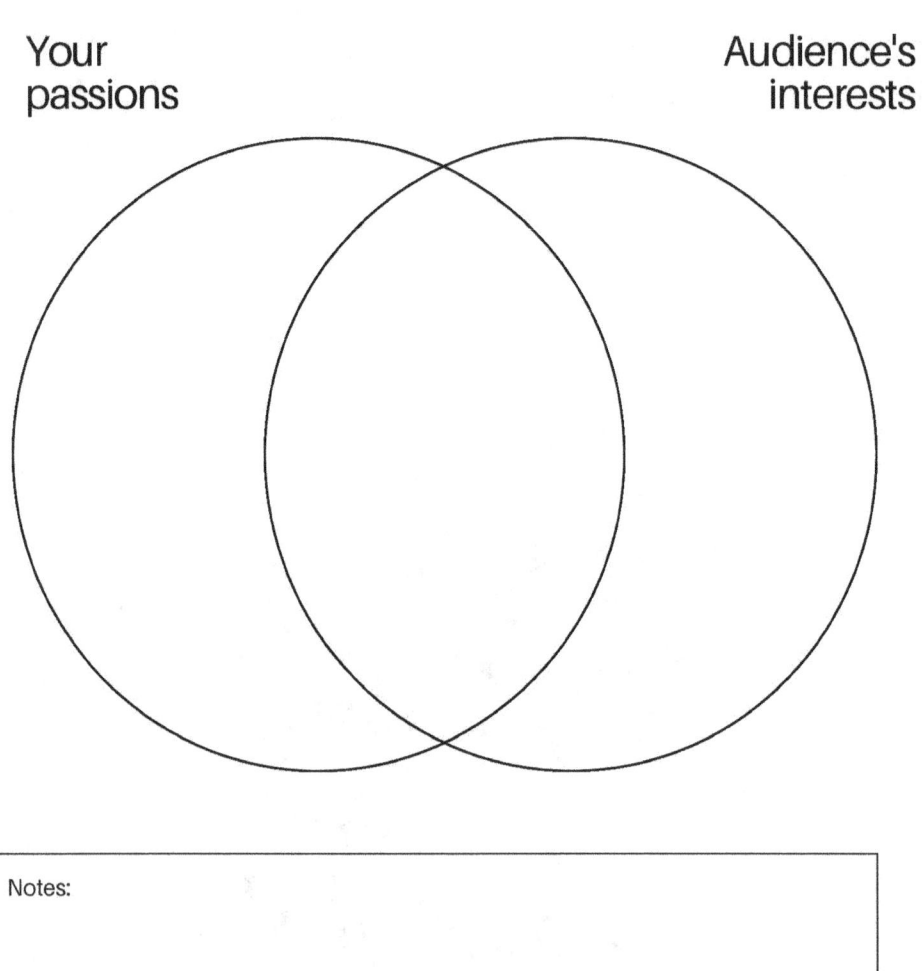

Your
passions

Audience's
interests

Notes:

Your Personal Brand

Define your core values and key characteristics that represent your brand.

Write your answer here...

Identify your unique style, voice, and visual elements that align with your brand.

Write your answer here...

Create a brand mood board or collage to visually represent your brand identity

Write a mission statement that encapsulates the essence of your brand.

Mission Statement Example:

"Our brand is dedicated to empowering individuals to unleash their creativity, share their unique stories, and inspire meaningful connections. Through captivating content and authentic experiences, we aim to ignite passion, spark curiosity, and create a positive impact in the lives of our audience."

Write your answer here...

**Chapter 5:
Crafting Your
Personal Brand**

**Your Adventure
Awaits: Conquer the
Digital Frontier**

Create an elevator pitch that effectively captures the mission of your brand.

Elevator Pitch:

"At [Brand Name], we are passionate about fostering creativity and connecting with others through compelling content. We strive to inspire and empower individuals to embrace their authentic selves, explore new perspectives, and embark on a transformative journey. Join us as we create a vibrant community where creativity knows no bounds."

Write your answer here...

Selecting
Suitable
Platforms

Research and compare different online platforms such as social media, blogs, and video-sharing sites.

Write your answer here...

Evaluate each platform's features, target audience, and engagement levels.

Write your answer here...

Consider your content type, format, and audience preferences to determine the most suitable platforms.

Create a pros and cons list for each platform to make an informed decision.

Platform	Pros	Cons

Chapter 7:
Creating High-Quality
Content

Creating
Content

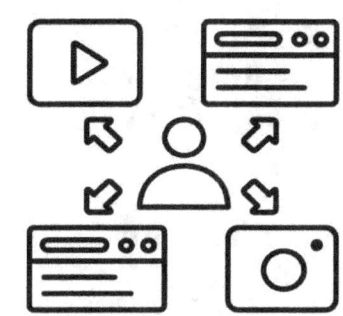

Define the purpose and goals of your content.

Write your answer here...

Research and study successful content creators in your niche.

Write your answer here...

Chapter 7:
Creating High-Quality Content

Practice Your Skills

Engage in deliberate practice by consistently creating content across various mediums such as writing compelling articles, capturing stunning photographs, and producing captivating videos, allowing you to hone your skills, experiment with different techniques, and discover your unique creative voice.

Seek feedback

Embrace a growth mindset by actively seeking constructive feedback from respected individuals in your field or engaging with online communities dedicated to content creation, enabling you to gain valuable insights, identify areas for improvement, and elevate the overall quality and impact of your content.

Resources

- Explore online courses, tutorials, or books that cover content creation techniques and best practices.
- Join workshops or webinars led by experts in your chosen content format.
- Utilize editing tools and software specific to your content medium

Notes:

Chapter 8:

EXTRAS

A comprehensive list of digital tools
&
30 Day Content Media Planner

Chapter 8:

Here's a comprehensive list of digital tools and resources that will be invaluable for anyone reading "Mastering Online Content Creation: A Comprehensive Workbook for Aspiring Creators":

Content Planning and Organization

- Trello - Project management tool for organizing content ideas and planning schedules.

- Asana - Task management software to streamline content creation workflows.

- Notion - All-in-one workspace for notes, tasks, and project planning.

- Google Calendar - Scheduling tool to keep track of content deadlines and publishing dates.

Writing and Editing

- Grammarly - Writing assistant for grammar and style checking.

- Hemingway Editor - Tool to improve readability and conciseness in writing.

- Scrivener - Comprehensive writing software for drafting and organizing long-form content.

- Google Docs - Collaborative word processor for creating and sharing documents.

SEO and Analytics

- Google Analytics - Tool for tracking and analyzing website traffic and user behavior.

- Ahrefs - SEO toolset for keyword research, competitor analysis, and site audits.

- SEMrush - All-in-one marketing toolkit for SEO, PPC, and content marketing.

- Moz - SEO software for keyword research and site optimization.

Collaboration and Communication

- Slack - Communication tool for team collaboration.

- Zoom - Video conferencing tool for virtual meetings and webinars.

- Microsoft Teams - Collaboration platform with chat, video conferencing, and file sharing.

- Dropbox - Cloud storage service for sharing and collaborating on files.

Email Marketing

- Mailchimp - Email marketing platform for creating and managing campaigns.

- ConvertKit - Email marketing tool tailored for content creators and bloggers.

- AWeber - Email marketing software for creating and automating email sequences.

- Sendinblue - Comprehensive email marketing and automation tool.

Audio Production and Editing

- Audacity - Free, open-source audio editing software.

- Adobe Audition - Professional audio editing and mixing software.

- GarageBand - Audio production software for Mac users, great for beginners.

- Anchor - Podcast creation and hosting platform.

Graphic Design and Visual Content

- Canva - User-friendly graphic design tool for creating social media graphics, presentations, and more.

- Adobe Creative Cloud - Suite of professional design tools, including Photoshop, Illustrator, and InDesign.

- Piktochart - Tool for creating infographics and visual reports.

- Unsplash - Resource for high-quality, royalty-free images.

Video Creation and Editing

- Adobe Premiere Pro - Professional video editing software.

- Final Cut Pro - Advanced video editing software for Mac users.

- iMovie - Beginner-friendly video editing software for Mac users.

- DaVinci Resolve - Professional-grade video editing and color correction tool.

E-commerce and Monetization

- Shopify - E-commerce platform for setting up online stores.

- WooCommerce - WordPress plugin for adding e-commerce functionality to your website.

- Patreon - Platform for creators to monetize their content through memberships.

- Teachable - Tool for creating and selling online courses.

Web Hosting and CMS

- WordPress - Popular content management system for building and managing websites.

- Squarespace - Website builder with elegant templates and easy-to-use tools.

- Wix - User-friendly website builder with drag-and-drop functionality.

- Bluehost - Web hosting service with easy WordPress integration.

These tools and resources will equip aspiring content creators with everything they need to plan, create, manage, and promote their content effectively.

30 DAY SOCIAL MEDIA CONTENT PLANNER

MONTH
_____

1 Founding story	2 Behind the scenes	3 Product or service of the day	4 Question of the day	5 Customer testimonials
6 Discounts and promotions	7 Industry news	8 Ways to use the product/service	9 Meet the team	10 Quote of the day
11 Contests and awards	12 Problem-solving tips	13 Funny moments at work	14 Industry meetings	15 Year in review
16 Product/service comparison	17 Production behind the scenes	18 User guides	19 Greetings from the team	20 Themed series
21 Polls and surveys	22 Photo of the day	23 Industry reflections	24 Thank yous	25 Expert advice
26 Tutorial videos	27 Motivational content	28 Famous customers	29 Environmental solutions	30 Request for feedback

30 DAY
SOCIAL MEDIA
CONTENT PLANNER

MONTH _____

Chapter 8:
The End
Conclusion

Congratulations on completing this comprehensive workbook for aspiring online content creators! Throughout this journey, you have gained valuable insights, acquired practical skills, and developed a strategic mindset to thrive in the dynamic world of online content creation.

Remember, becoming a successful online content creator is a continuous learning process. Embrace experimentation, adapt to changes in the digital landscape, and remain open to new possibilities. Your unique voice and creative expression have the power to make a profound impact on your audience and the online community.

Stay true to your passions, values, and personal brand

Never forget that creating content online is not just about sharing your ideas but also about connecting with others, inspiring, educating, and entertaining. Embrace the responsibility and privilege that comes with having a platform, and use it to spread positivity and make a difference.

Remember, you have the potential to become a standout online content creator. Embrace the challenges, learn from setbacks, and let your creativity shine. Your unique perspective and authentic voice will captivate and inspire your audience.

Best of luck!

Maria Davila

BOOK RELEASE

DONATE TO
DISASTER RELIEF

WRITTEN BY MARIA DAVILA

SUICIDE
LETTERS

LET ME
WRITE
YOUR
BOOK

Self Publish
Your Book In
2025

BRAND YOUR
BUSINESS

FOLLOW ME HERE!